# The Long Answer

New & Selected Poems

**Also by David Keplinger**

*The Rose Inside* (Truman State University Press, 1999)

*The Clearing* (New Issues, 2005)

*The Prayers of Others* (New Issues, 2006)

*World Cut out with Crooked Scissors: The Selected Poetry of Carsten René Nielsen* [translations from the Danish] (New Issues, 2007)

*By & By* [eleven songs] (Morphius Records, 2011)

*House Inspections* [Nielsen: translations from the Danish] (BOA Editions Ltd, 2011)

*The Most Natural Thing* (New Issues, 2013)

*The Art of Topiary: The Selected Poetry of Jan Wagner* [translations from the German] (Milkweed Editions, 2017)

*Another City* (Milkweed Editions, 2018)

*Forty-One Objects* [Nielsen: translations from the Danish] (Bitter Oleander, 2019)

"Imagine *The Inferno* reconfigured as a cross between one of Joseph Cornell's boxes and a Rube Goldberg drawing: an infernal machine designed to produce the uncomfortable pleasures of wit's disjunctions, gallows humor, wry nostalgias…What's consistent is the sustained invention of a tinkerer who takes his materials (so many of them fragile, easily discarded or mislaid) to heart even as he finds his humor, his consolation in the spirited play of their arrangements."

*The Antioch Review*

"…The book's meditations on mortality and wounded dissatisfaction are equally haunted by metaphysical longing and the vast otherworld in the near at hand. To arrive in a body, through the body of another, is to feel its suffering as the echo, however distant, of our own. In poems of such keen attentions and imaginative wit, the intimation of always another city registers both an awareness of our inevitable diminishment and the possibility of some vaster sphere, some landscape of domes and illuminations, to mitigate our loneliness and loss."

Judges' citation, 2019 UNT Rilke Prize

"His prose is so well-crafted and compact that you'd think they wrote themselves into the world—that they were born complete and right on their due date, with no complications …Keplinger's collection is stunning and visceral."

-*The Rumpus*

Keplinger's poems, by juxtaposing such disintegration or failure to an integrated aesthetic that does *not* fail…ultimately [succeed] at precisely those moments where they take the most risk.…A tender, graceful, and profound meditation on the ways in which we experience our bodies in the world; shuttling expertly between the narrative and the lyric, the ordinary and the wild, the book asks us to envision the body as that lived intersection between, as Keplinger would have it, the natural and the natural."

-*Triquarterly*

"The question is less whether Keplinger benefits from the prose poem than whether prose poetry benefits from Keplinger—a question [his poetry] answers with a resounding yes."

-*The American Book Review*

# *The Long Answer*

New & Selected Poems

## DAVID KEPLINGER

STEPHEN F. AUSTIN STATE UNIVERSITY PRESS

Copyright © 2020 by Stephen F. Austin State University Press

All rights reserved
First Edition
Printed in the United States of America

For information about permission to reproduce selections from this book, contact *permissions* :

Stephen F. Austin State University Press
P.O. Box 13007, SFA Station
Nacogdoches, TX 75962
sfapress@sfasu.edu
www.sfasu.edu/sfapress
936-468-1078

Project Manager: Kimberly Verhines
Assistant Editor: Tristan Brewster
Cover Art: Jim Youngerman, Untitled Tryptych, from *Lonesome Landscape* series 6' x 18" 1995, jimyoungerman.com

ISBN: 978-1-62288-308-0

First Edition

*For Amy, caster of bread upon waters*
and
*For Bobbi, huckleberry friend*

# Table of Contents

**FROM: *THE ROSE INSIDE* (1999)**
Blessing for the Liver  ⬖  15
The House at Graterford Prison  ⬖  16
Last Days in America  ⬖  18
The Distance between Zero and One  ⬖  19
The Dove  ⬖  20
*From:* Lineage  ⬖  21
On Vicolo San Lorenzo I See My Family Name  ⬖  23
San Calogero Healing Springs  ⬖  24

**FROM: *THE CLEARING* (2005)**
View from Outside  ⬖  27
Lorca's Passport  ⬖  28
Elegy for the Precious Time before Dinner  ⬖  29
Cortez Arrives at San Juan de Ulloa  ⬖  30
Our Secret Icarus Is  ⬖  31
Instructions for the Lost  ⬖  32
Max Jacob at Abby St. Benoit sur Loire  ⬖  33
Basic Training  ⬖  34
Darwin Remembers the Island of Chiloe  ⬖  36
The North  ⬖  38
Three Visions of the Peril of Art  ⬖  39
*From:* Correspondences  ⬖  40
Waking on the Pribor Train, Near Freud's Birthplace  ⬖  42
Pig Slaughter  ⬖  43
Side Work  ⬖  45
View from Inside  ⬖  46

**FROM: *THE PRAYERS OF OTHERS* (2006)**
"I stood too close"  ⬖  49
"On the first"  ⬖  50
"Life on Earth"  ⬖  51
"Walking by myself"  ⬖  52
"The little girl"  ⬖  53
"Where I should"  ⬖  54

"Could this be Satan"  55
"How many sparrows"  56
"Time is moving exactly"  57
"Adam's"  58
"Eve stands"  59
"The ear's an earthy garden"  60
"I am an actor"  61
"Venus"  62
"The hiddenness of God"  63
"I could see the clock"  64
"We stripped"  65
"In her hospital bed"  66
"I've been to this station"  67
"I made this"  68

FROM: *THE MOST NATURAL THING* **(2013)**
Enormous Yellow Sky  71
The Assumption  72
In Translation: 1901  73
Slowness  74
In Messina  75
The Herd Gate Injury  76
The Dead in Certain Old Photographs  77
Whatever Sings Belongs to No one  78
Cilia  79
The Right Brain  80
A Day at Olesna  81
The Belly  82
The Heart  83
The Bladder  84
The Crown of Light at Assisi  85
Events Surrounding my Supposed Birth  86
The Pancreas  87
Sleepwalking  88
The Unicorn in Modern Memory  89
The Sleepers  90
In Translation: Woe-Mood  91
Max Jacob's Prayer List at Drancy  92

"May I See What You Are"   93
Fat   94
Gender Study   95
The Most Natural Thing   96
Removal   97

FROM: *ANOTHER CITY* **(2018)**
City of Birth   101
Carp   102
Chance   103
Q: In What City Does Your Mother Live?   104
Ardor   105
Preservation   106
The Liquid R   107
Hymn   108
My Town   109
Letter from Rock Creek   110
Calling Horses   111
"An Apartment in the City of Death"   112
Wave   113
A Young Man's Copybook   114
Comet   119
Beatification   120
"Marie Curie's Century Old Radioactive Notebook Still   122
    Requires Lead Box"
Lovesickness   123
X, & Axe   124
Embarrassment   126
The Leatherback   127
The Sibilant   128
A Blue Dish   129
The Little Stairs of Z   130
My Father's Hours   131
My Carnation   132
Magic   133
"Every Angel is Terrifying"   134
Empire, Discourse   135

ON THREE (New Poems)
Composition for Three Voices: A Tenement in Moravia   139
Hieronymous Bosch's Self-Portrait in Hell   141
222 West Twenty-Third Street   143
Composition for the Faith of Clifford Brown   144
The Dice Cup   146
Pearl Street   147
Three Close Readings in a Darkening Time   152
Justice, Three Panels   155
Pictures of my Family   157
Only the Marvelous is Beautiful   158
Theory   162
My Solitude   163
With Rilke in the Josefhov Quarter   164
Sonnet   165
Eulogy after a Convalescence   166
The Long Answer   167


Acknowledgments   169

From: *THE ROSE INSIDE* (1999)

## Blessing for the Liver

The heart with its lies
is perched in blue branches, neither

dangerous nor kind,
the serpent, the lonely.

And the brain is where
the world once fell

from the smallest tree in the orchard,
the apple my great-grandfather

carves with a razor for eternity,
twirling it in his hands

to eat, the delectable
fruit we are too much of.

But cut the liver from my body intact,
which faced all my poisons.

No wonder it's the bearer of the soul,
stone at the end of my life.

# The House at Graterford Prison

1.
Saltweed in the garden, overhanging, banal.
    She, in the house, shucks
corn at the sink overlooking the field.
The hush of wind, *The people are sad,* the child says
*Those people are already smoke,* filtering from their cell windows at night
        corn silk falling away in the basin

2.
The child saw a dragonfly hovering
in the tall grass before the field:

if it was real, its wings were black-veined,
metal contraptions.

If he had words he'd say it's all amiss,
that he and this thing are together

in the world. From this point on
he will feel improbable: a thousand cracked mirrors

in the blacks and yellows will tell him so, the cruel
myopia of its inner eye.


3.
She guts catfish, heart,
    liver, string of intestine, pieces
she can't quite name, takes
    in her hand the smell of sex,

the backbone peeled
    away. The child doesn't like
the taste but catches them
    in the stagnant

pools below the bridges
    of the Perkiomen. Here's
where he pried the hook
    from the eye, the half eye—

4.
Fire came down to him.
    In sleep it whispered
*Destroy what I have made*,
    from blade of grass to rose,

weed, and animate things:
    the blue speckled egg
whose filling comes to life
    huddled and wet in the yolk;

and the serpent didn't escape
    whose skin turns to ash,
translucent, nor his counterpart
    the waterstrider, whom he

scooped from the surface
    of the pond that afternoon
where it glided in boring light,
    and burned in the corn

the crackling feelers curling under a match.

## Last Days in America

We spent the last days fishing off the dam.
Simple living minnow, circling in a bucket,
I lifted you out with my hands.
Your tiny mouth parted. The hook slipped down your throat
and out the belly.

# The Distance between Zero and One

In April the carnival came.
The ice and the factory lot,
the carnival rides huffing black stripes of smoke.

Pig slaughter music.
Veronika stirring the blood with her hands.
Others cleaning the long blue
intestines in snowdrifts
filled with tiny stones.

## The Dove

Days the crowds emerge at three pm

in September performers emerge with their stands—

the doves unfold like paper
in a street magician's hands—

and the new money is good for bread
and the old money for salt, yeast, sugar

The old money in one pocket, the new in the other

On the table we keep a dictionary: it takes minutes for Nika to say
*You are tender* and me back: you are tender

The bath, the white tub, Turkish coffee on a white chair
For a long while

I've been too fast to talk, I should take my time

with words, the words are precious

An hour for the coffee on the fire

A dove

*From:* Lineage

I KNOW what I know is uncommon.
Why do you think I'm so happy?
I make a shadow with my hands.
It makes no sense.

Did you ever see his shadow in the dark?
Did you ever see God's little shadow?
I press my hands together.
It makes no sense.

\*

ON THE TABLE, a statue of Mary,
surrounded by starlings,
a novena to Saint Jude
to be said for nine days.

It was me who put that rose
inside your body. Geese squawking
a slow adagio. Dawn. The moon
written out in chalk.

\*

THE LAST SIN I committed
was naming the serpent.
I saw it in the tree,
coiled in its shroud.

I tried to let the tongue's split root
speak for itself, but don't you agree
the sound is hissing? Don't you agree
*Snake* is its body

as it lurches through jonquils
in theorems of thought?
Oh equal proportion, of god
of equations, oh fine way

the jaw unlatches to swallow an egg.


\*


MY BAD EYE crosses.
It turns my face toward
pitiable, the off-balanced
gleam of the imbecile:

eye in its nothing pose,
drifting out of orbit.
The rest was easy. The tumor tears
in half, begins again,

and the work is good.
The molecule deviates.
The body vanishes.
The work is good.

## On Vicolo San Lorenzo, I See My Family Name

A little waterfront not on the map.
The small blue boats with tires for life rafts
float along the dock,
where fishermen gather mornings.
A salamander skitters up the oar
and steals inside a tiny crack
between my eyelashes.
Four boats,
moored beneath the statue of Mary,
covered with lichens and gulls.
I want to think I'm someone else
but I'm always right here in my body,
my America. Here in my palm,
too small to be a fisherman's,
an aquamarine wave
has come a long way
to rend itself.

## San Calogero Healing Springs

Under a canopy
    of ivy, the Christ,
with iron nails

    the iron worker
hammered, hangs
    loose on the bow

of his ivory spine
    where the grotto opens.
It is morning here.

    The old nun
sweeps a courtyard
    with a black straw broom

that fans out
    like palm leaves
and does little good.

    Piled behind her
the pyramid of lemons
    remains standing,

marvelously,
    in the sunlight.

From: *THE CLEARING* (2005)

## View from Outside

From which all things spray violent and out
there is a point of singularity.
In Michelangelo's sculpture of the heart,
for instance, the heart wears the costume
of David's body. In the eyes of the Judean
there isn't any fear of what the heart has made.
When I died, I could see from that perspective,
how something mute sat like a stone inside
the clenching and unclenching of my heart.
I had the stone. Only it would pay attention.

## Lorca's Passport

In the photograph,
which we know
the poet admired,
which we know
he called *spiritualistic*,
the vague,
spotted bow tie
like a moth
has come to rest
slightly crooked
at his throat.
His shirt glows,

the visible portion
an upside down
triangle or a lily
that has opened
to bear his head
from the dark
of the charcoal
buttoned shirt.
One eye
is shadowed. One ear
is black, sucked
into his hair.

The ear we can see
is a luminous egg.
There is a pinprick
in the center.
The other eye's socket
swallows his pupil
like a moat. "It borders
on the light
of murder,"
he once wrote of it.
"Over my shoulder,
a sort of harp…"

## Elegy for the Precious Time before Dinner

Along the fringe of two known worlds
of field, of prison yard,
behind the house my mother and her sisters
live in, this was years ago.

We're all still there, itinerant
as wind, the straits of corn
and prison guards who pace their impossible promontories
and the small mouse just born into this world,
total as a thumb.

With her sisters who are dead, my mother is a beauty
taking the spoon
to beat the dog away from the pot
at which they all begin to laugh.

Little beetles with a kind of Viking armor
I want to smash you, smash the spiders
atop their pagodas
like bad thoughts,
smash the crazy locust who won't abandon its post.

At the house the women happily
eye up the sauce about to boil.
I am wearing my emblematic cape.
I can fly at any moment if I want to,
but I don't.

## Cortez Arrives at San Juan de Ulloa

He belongs to no one now.
He trims his beard with tiny golden scissors. He whittles
at his fingertips.

Each shoulder in its armor, the willful potential
of a yolk. He fits his feet in stirrups.
He yanks the rotten tooth.

And this is Cortez in his boots: Lord of Death,
Lord of Fire, whose ship is burning, who spits and gives commands
into the air,

that he is never going back; to the one wave turning
on another; to that ash heap; that boat;
that murdering sea.

## Our Secret Icarus Is

A railway conductor
who sells coffee to his passengers.

He should be demanding the tickets.
He should be
scolding the passengers
who flounder at the station
with their goodbyes.
He should be pulling them in by the arms.

Ladies and gentlemen
let's drink a little Russian vodka and be patient now.
He's on his way with a hole in his pocket
and no change
ringing his little bell.

His cups of coffee are sodden with grounds.
He spills them handing them over.
He can't interpret what's left
as a sign.

The math, he says,
is beyond him.

## Instructions for the Lost

Above the cellars
lined with preserves,
in a foreign year,

its calendar girls
naked except for
their parasols,

you may find that you are lost.
You may listen
to the gurgle

of the small red chimneys
filling up with dark.
Into that dark

that sleeves the bare branches
like a heavy sack,
a crow will disappear, children.

Pay attention to the crow.
The windpipe
with its tiny rungs.

## Max Jacob at Abbey St. Benoit-sur-Loire

The poem grabs him by the nape:
the sullen French, their howitzers' largess
somewhere near Petite Pierre, a passage
like the horrors of his sleep.
Fey and inattentive at the Abbey,
he twiddles in his pin-stripe with the monks.
He fills the heat-soft pages of his books.
He kneads his mound of bread all day.
He knows a garret where the devil feeds;
a little flop on Rue St. Paul; an alley
for the damned. He tries to pray.
But it's no good: the French are dead.
It's 1926. Lost without their war,
statues and police sulk everywhere.

## Basic Training

He sits on the Greyhound bus.
Just below the window
where the driver smokes,
the year is 1955.

He's on his way to basic training.
The father sells insurance
and has been on strike
and has time

to take his son to the station.
He has time
to make a little
chit chat. He talks about

some money he has made
selling rare coins.
He talks to his son
from the street.

The passing traffic
shakes the Greyhound bus.
The father lights a cigarette
and gazes towards

some small, indefinable point
on the horizon.
The son looks at it, too.
They look at it and look at it.

The son would like a cigarette.
He would like his father
to tell him what he sees.
But the father says

one more thing:
what was it? The other
will always have to wonder,
have to tell about,

like this,
as the bus shoves off;
and the door closes;
the enormous wing.

## Darwin Remembers the Island of Chiloe

Almost never did I get a view as clear
as that: dormant Cordillero,
as the sun came up, without the glare
or rain. After that, the work was slow
from plodding through the muck and scum.
I should have died before the ship turned home.

I didn't die. And never thought I would. Not ever.
Even in my sickness, or all alone
inside the bush, the metal taste
of vomit in my mouth. Is a man just a brain,
one chestnut spiked fruit in an endless wood?
Must the branches connect with each other?

November the tenth, the sea was full
of violence. Cordillero about to hide.
I sat inside the Beagle with the peat
and barking-birds. The food
did not agree with me. The stink of sheep
and wild potato rotting in the hull,

and the Chiloeans sick with worms.
They ate diseases from their quadrupeds.
They warned me how the spirits of the dead
inhabited my specimens of birds.
They prayed to God in angry outbursts.
They used the Christian terms.

I met some of them in a cave
one time, where they held service.
It was by some trick of fire I observed
a man transformed into a kind of bird
I couldn't name. Nature works by her devices;
What was her logic then? What should I believe?

The hot volcano rumbled, obscure again.
The bird snapped back into a man.
And I came back to notebooks on the Beagle
and the million years of history to wrestle,
and my ship's sad, nomadic walls.
And the future. And the apocalyptic sea.

## The North

The saddest trains go north.
Along the aisles
men hang in place.

They grasp the drooping wires
and try not to remember
their loneliness.

The women sit. They wave,
they move their hands
like through water. They clutch

their purses and square hats.
They are so busy, they have no time
to ward off strangers.

When they come to a stop,
all bow forward like in a prayer.
The men unclench.

The women gather their things:
the hands of children still asleep
are heaviest.

Three Visions of the Peril of Art

*1. Childhood Home of Smetana*
The snowed-over tracks carried us
like Providence. We lived in an occupied country
before the wars. We were passing through his little town.
Smetana the Deaf once held rapt
Sudetan and Jew alike: they crowded in to hear him
at the National House. He called that music, "My Land."
The snow and the faces in the station hovered
over the bags on the platform. I was falling back asleep.
I dreamed of blaring sound that swallowed everything.

*2. Breughel's "Peasant Wedding"*
Because the groom is absent,
onlooker, you must be her groom. You are the missing
flash of life, a ghost, the happy guest of Flanders.
Go to this clearing in the woods
where the mushrooms are hiding and locusts
burst their prisons again and again. The woman
was married in the powerful stench of sugar
and beer. She wears a crown of peacock feathers,
a gown the color of shoes.

*3. The Story's Mine about My Mother*
"I want to suffer my own suffering
and die my own death," my mother wrote
into a book of poems I once gave her.
When I discovered them,
I felt those lines more lovingly
than any in the book. She told me once
and I believe her
that whatever I make with my own hands
is mine. The earth is sad and right, she also said.

*From*: Correspondences

*How the Brain Emerged from Water*

Chemical, mathematical, the brain was a fish. Now hold that kingdom in your hands. It wriggles out. It swallows almost anything. It stinks like its hook and its kin.


*How the Moth Became the Magpie*

The moth, his full beard coated with dust, knew he was dying, so what else? He began to cry. His own tears dissolved the delicate powder of his wings. The fall proved very long: the moon animated the lake, its white light flickering, and the grasses bent in the great wind that carried him. He was Colossus, the acrobat, lithe, lucky, far away, flying further out. His feathers were black, were white. His feathers were blue inside the wing. He was the colors of that lake in darkness.


*How the Mouth Emerged from Fire*

Negative organ, the mouth is a burnt-out hole, a tragedy worthy of fire. The tongue is the only survivor, deformed. The mouth yearns for alliances, the cold union of the body, the oligarchies of the fingers and toes. That's why it must be flushed with water all the time, because it smolders. Because it tastes of ashes, and still stings.


*How the Bat Became the Crow*

The empty hollow of an egg, bat's stomach. His skin felt sick. You know how, under the right conditions, when a person dies in the cold, the eyes and mouth withdraw, the skin loosens? Now the oily feathers punched through. Now he could hear, but with his eyes. A spider was falling out of the sky. He would never have to follow it again.

*How the Feet Emerged from Fire*

Though lifetimes swirl in the forever of these carbons, the story of the feet is brief. I have seen how infants hold the lick of the foot to their mouths. Succulent, delicious whorl of salt: an infant might like to return to you, but I do not.


*How the Crayfish Became the Waterstrider*

The crayfish had a kingdom, a stone. He had no brains to fear the dark he lived in. He lived there. He was born there. His face was indecipherable. His body was hard, impenetrable. He couldn't even remember how to move. One story goes like this. He remembered how to move. When he did, the kingdom toppled. That's how he discovered he'd been under water. Now he moves along the surface of the water, having everything.


*How the Heart Emerged from Fire*

The heart began as a point. It grazed the soapy rims of stars. It became a straight line. The atmosphere of earth was a scrappy land to find. My own heart, my tiny savant, goodnight. You sleep with your eyes wide open, the skin of the body pulled over your head.

## Waking on the Pribor Train, Near Freud's Birthplace

I hear before I see.
Halfway through the rain-wet
fields of Pribor in winter,
some distant, barking dogs
suggest the town.
I have heard tell
of its shops with names
predating the war
when this was a Jewish city.
I have found it all this way
like a cup or a pocketknife
or a hat from childhood
I thought was lost.
Illumined by the station lights
the tiny veins
flicker behind my eyes
and I open my eyes:
it's like floating back into the world
after prayer. The moon
is out. The dogs are slick
and fluid in their tight, black fur.

## Pig Slaughter

Whatever house
    would host the slaughter,
stunk of death. The hurdle
    worst to cross

was the killing:
    the butcher
with his butcher's gun
    got himself acquainted

with the pig.
    The pig has knowledge
too; the pig is kind
    or cruel, depending;

it winces like a man
    before it's shot.
The happy butcher
    slung it to the ladder

standing upright
    at the house, and from the neck
he sliced the dead,
    delicious skin.

Then into drums
    pumped all its life.
Someone stirred the blood
    by bare hand,

someone scooping
    barley stuffed the barley
into intestine, blue
    and scoured in snow.

The rest is tenderness.
    The cooking of the pig
is like no quiet
    I have known.

## Side Work

Great things begin
in the periphery.
Meanwhile my father

works third shift
at the mustard plant.
He's around my age.

He's finished
for the night.
He revs his truck,

waiting for the heat.
The ladder shakes
in its rack on top.

The heat is dusty,
coming on. All this
can happen

without us, just
out of view:
It's almost morning.

The smallest tools
begin to shudder now
in their boxes.

## View from Inside

To teach me how to use the scythe,
Standa held his two hands over mine.
Beside my body he guided my body
through the high grass. Like this.

By dark we had made a little clearing.
You're doing very well, he said.
I couldn't see a thing. I just kept looking up
ahead and swinging, like I do this.

From: *THE PRAYERS OF OTHERS* (2006)

I STOOD TOO CLOSE to the lion cage and was eaten right up. My mother called and called for me. I landed in the lion's gut, and the gut was melted butter, its kills strung high along the cursive of its vertebrae. When the lion breathed in deeply, they flapped. I named this purring.

ON THE FIRST level of Hell with Paolo and Francesca sits Max Jacob. You had no choices, Francesca says to Paolo. You had no choices, says the other to the other. Jacob in his dirty pin stripe suit just laughs and laughs at them. He has a brief affair with one of Darwin's finches. She visits only at night. She permits him to stroke the yellowish down of her breast, which occasionally he reads by.

LIFE ON EARTH is pulled down hard on a man's head. This life was made by hatters. A busy street is only coffee, bread, and hats. The smell of a man's hat, an old man's hat, is like the nostril of a horse. You are breathing in what something *more* than you has breathed completely out. You are breathing silk interior; heat and life. An old man's hat is necessary. You see that when he takes it off, the hair and skin abruptly float away.

WALKING BY MYSELF through cities I think of knives, the symbol of marriages and doom. Or I recall the lucky spoons my auntie loved and hung on a rack by the table. She did not love her knives. They lay in a drawer. My auntie ripped her bread by hand. She said a knife is almost useless, being one thing only.

THE LITTLE GIRL has turned away her eyes, covered up her face as if ashamed. In this picture, she has chanced upon a rotting cow. The giant teeth exposed, its mouth has burned away like film burns slowly in a theater. Her shadow darkens the scrap of fur in the shape of Texas, matted against the belly of the thing. The cow seems to gleam with wetness like turf in darkness. It all manages to fetch—perhaps because of the angle of the sun or the invisible photographer, or the horror of the girl—the effect that the cow is smiling, a perfectly content dead animal.

WHERE I SHOULD have come to Judas impaled by huge incisors, instead I discovered Antonin Artaud, still writing his manifesto, "To Finish with the Judgment of God." All his teeth were pulled. It was so quiet there, I even heard the scratching of his pen. He had no jacket for the long approaching winter. A kind of dog had chewed his hands and feet.

COULD THIS BE SATAN, whose drop from Heaven made this hole? I thought to myself. It was a tiny child, hanging by four straps, like the heart suspended in its branches. That baby's just a memory. My mother had left me to swing in the shade.

*"Where knowledge and desire end, there is darkness, and there God shines."*
—Meister Eckhart

HOW MANY SPARROWS am I worth? A sparrow of the kingdom *Animalia*, of the *Aves* class, stood on its equals sign, my mother's double clothesline. It stood between my window and the prison with its twinkling searchlights, stood foraging for seed and maggots in the coarse, sweating grass of history. I held a sparrow once. I saw no difference from one of Darwin's finches. With its stout unending chest, supercilium in bold, the curtness of its beak and brains. Light who clothes me, I ask you.

TIME IS MOVING EXACTLY at the pace a little girl can read by candlelight. And when she mouths the words, running her fingers under the words as she speaks them, tadpoles burst into frogs, a liver regenerates, flesh rises off the body as a fleck of dust. She never stops, except when her eyes get tired, and that's when I notice silence.

ADAM's on the right, his name is Red Earth. His face is burned, as if made of ash. He lies on his back on the sand, a tree growing out of his sex. The tree contains all metals known to us. The branches spread like veins into the dirt and cities and the rivers of the world. He gives us choice: to be the anvil or the sword.

EVE STANDS on the left. Her belly, pouched, is a pelican's mouth. She is neither mercurial nor shy. She clasps a fish in one hand, a cloud in the other. Look closely now: the fish is not a fish. Above her are the sun and moon, even in the sky. Her cloud is full of lightning bolts that strike like serpents touching mouths.

THE EAR'S AN EARTHY GARDEN with its own forbidden tree. God still walks there leisurely in the cool of the evening. The tree has never been discovered. That's why the garden stinks of rinds; the swells of full fruit thudding in our heads. "The porches of my ears," Dead Hamlet called its tiny gate, its nautilus design, where someone's often whistling.

I AM AN ACTOR playing myself, watching my grandfather down the road. He is an actor, too, the most distinguished of them all. He wants to speak. The words barely flicker on his throat's wick. *Write it down, write it down*, I tell him. I hold this man by the thick of the arm, its muscle of wool. And he exits: he and his small white papers.

VENUS is a ball of gas that, underneath, has mountains like the Catskills. The only blessed souls that live there are Romantic poets and, in special cases, toxic frogs, St. George's dragon, and the angel whose job it is to visit us in dreams. The angel would like to give the job to Keats, who is too busy taking labored breaths into his handkerchief.

*"Wherever anything lives, there is, open somewhere, a register in which time is being inscribed."*
—Henri Bergson

THE HIDDENNESS OF GOD is necessary. God hides within the space between a thing and other things. Without this space, we have no urge to go forth, and we are here to go forth. I discovered at my death there is no space between. God is not hidden. There is no going forth.

I COULD SEE THE CLOCK from any angle in the house: but regardless where I stood it told a different time. From the window, the clock appeared an hour slow. By the door it was fast. If I woke up in the middle of the night and walked into the darkness in the hall, it had no hands, though I could hear it, clearly ticking through the hollows of the rooms.

WE STRIPPED and swam to the Green Island. It was earliest summer. There is such a thing as midnight sun. Asa let me touch her from behind, her body so much older than mine. Under water she yelled something—what? I don't remember. What we call sorrow is merely failing memory.

IN HER HOSPITAL BED, my mother drinks her water from a plastic cup. They have stolen me under her coats so I can visit her. They've made a show of this. She sits straight and strong in her chair. Memory's like skipping stones. I'm in the lobby with my Coke. I'm carried to the room where light pours in. Her face as blurry snapshot when she smiles from under her handkerchief.

I'VE BEEN TO THIS STATION, but I will never go back. A woman in a green gown was clasping a shoe to her ankle. The stiletto on that shoe the length of my pointer finger. The other foot was bare. The woman stood up, threw her purse on the crook of her shoulder. *Tik-tump, tik-tump*, and away she went. The train pulled out. Tell me, what shall I do with that image? She walks on the stilt of my finger.

I MADE THIS paper boat for her, who finds it difficult to sleep. She imagines she is floating on its little stern, here, under her sleeping mask, under the covers. All you'll need is one plain sheet. It's folded like the beak of an archaic bird. With your fingers, pry the wide beak open. You are opening the beak. You are climbing inside.

From: *THE MOST NATURAL THING* (2013)

*What is this enigmatic impulse that does not allow one to settle down in the achieved, the finished? I think it is the quest for reality.*
                                                            Czeslaw Milosz

## Enormous Yellow Sky

The same as everyone, I hunted for mushrooms before I was born, beneath the tarot flatness of a yellow sky. These were the woods where one meets the deer, the goddess in disguise. This is her symbol: what is hidden would like to be known. She led me to a banquet in a clearing. Several guests sat talking at a long table. "Soon no one alive will remember the eighteenth century," whispered my father into my mother's ear. "One day all this too will be a fairy tale," said my mother from behind her carnival mask.

## The Assumption

From its pellet-like source the universe widens. Our car broke down near the fairgrounds that winter. There I once saw the World's Tallest Man, harrowed by his ankyloses. He sat in a chair waving at us. Then he rose as if climbing a rope. Five o'clock, just about dark. The tow truck arrived. It cranked down its hook on a chain. It hoisted the bumper, lip of a fish, almost vertical. All together we climbed in the truck. The father, the son, the quiet driver.

In Translation: 1901

Her nickname will be Little Bread, after the bread she brings for lunch. First day of school, she comes without English, as though the dog has eaten it. When Teacher asks her name, she holds up her lunch, a little bread. Which makes them all laugh. She pokes two eyes in that roll, folds the bald dolly in her napkin, stuffs it in her coat. It's perfectly clear, she's come unprepared for the twentieth century. You can tell by the sepia tone in her skin, and her hair so tangled, it will have to be shaved.

## Slowness

The slow boy bats his swimming hands out in the reservoir. His mother, slow to admit his impediments, has let him go too deep, and he lunges, sucked into her egg of light. I've been a peasant all my life. I tear the bread. I eat too quickly. I rush the prayer at table. In this frame before his drowning, the universe is slow, and I want to be fast. The mother shows her worry now. She lifts her hand, cups it completely over the sun. The swimmer bats in furious wheels but comes no closer, embarrassed by this slowness he is learning.

## In Messina

In Messina, mottled rocks suggest the faces of small children, elated by their missing teeth. As if there'd be no end to solitude, the sea below Messina keeps insisting *solitude is beauty, you will not be lonely in your life*, but you are getting cold, so you return to your hotel, just as the light begins a change, at every stage more difficult to navigate. And when you look back into the rocks their toothless faces are no longer young; but old, confused—Then in Messina it's completely dark.

## The Herd Gate Injury

The herd gate didn't tear the shoulder from the neck, it tore the neck from the shoulder, and the neck was displaced in a far-flung angle. They carried him toward the feedlot. And all the way he was quiet. He held his hand against the neck. He did it to keep it from falling off the world, which is to say, he did it to keep it from falling off his body. To the feedlot he floated as toward a drawbridge. I'll pay for the gate, he managed at last. In careful English. I'll pay for everything I did and I am very sorry.

## The Dead in Certain Old Photographs

The rich at Fleury are covered in flowers; the servants lie buried in oak tree roots. So it is discovered when one tree is dug up, using shovels and picks in the flash of yellow sepia. At this exhumation it is 1920. The modern swimmers watch unselfconscious in bloomers and high-fitting trunks, drinking young wine from flutes and talking, laughing, shushing each other. The woman named Asa, who is not from this country, falls backwards in the water, maybe drunk. As she does, her hair fans into a brown corona.

## Whatever Sings Belongs to No one

Our singing girl turns three, sings to herself, blows the candles by herself. Whatever sings belongs to no one, she still knows, so sing, the idea is to sing, keep singing, then never let them make you stop. Does she already hear the peripheral doubts, does she see us yet, the terror figures she'll become? She wants to flee us in her minuscule car, singing, the cast from last month's accident already too small for her hand. She waves three fingers through the cast. I see a wolf mouth, swallowing the tail of a bird.

# Cilia

I am taken to surgery, they say cancer in my lung. The surgeon is Anicka, eyes smiling behind her mask. Then I dissolve in the loam of sleep. She discovers a tree she calls a *smrk*, branching upward in the darkness of my windpipe. She must give the tree back like a gift. Uprooted, it sits on the tip of her finger. To grow a *smrk*, the lung must be tar-sore and black. In Czech the word for death is *smrt*. Not the tree, but how the "t" moves back into Anicka's mouth, is the miraculous thing.

## The Right Brain

To activate it, strict codes of conduct were applied. Tiny John Keats wore ruffles and a jacket, slacks with a ribbon of satin hemmed up to his size. There's Dickinson's gown, apocryphal, bleached, and Blake's scratched lucky boots, his feet dunked in them. I have heard of Hart Crane's drinking blouse, its collar wound with an ascot; the cloak and tri-cornered hat of Marianne Moore; Pound's shabby trousers; the fly is down. It's Saturday night. We've all had our baths. We dress ourselves in our uniforms. For this.

# A Day at Olesna

We are right here. We are in this water. From the water I lift up my hand. Then comes the feeling of being in time, of being here always, of waiting for my hand to rise and for my mind to look at it. Can all that happened have been real? Your hair pulled back into a ponytail, it floats spread out, feathered, on the lake. We are here. At last we are in water. The water beads on top of your shoulders. In the waves I sway like a suicide. Your hand in the air like a flag. Your ribs slip under.

## The Belly

I fell into my mother's purse, and out shut the world with a snap. Then there I was, coming to, among her lipstick tubes, box of Chiclets, the leather gloves, full pack of Parliaments. Death smelled of mint and décolleté. No crow was going to come to peck the artery of this whale and free me from my loneliness, sealed up good, with very little air to last. There was a feeling of such power (I was a special child), it got the best of me. I made my throne out of the compact puff. I ruled by my scepter, the unlit match.

## The Heart

The morning before his open-heart surgery my father and I drive to Elmwood Park Zoo. But no one greets us at the gate. The stalls for the animals are suddenly gone, the zoo defunct. I think of the giraffes somewhere munching on trees, feeding on anything that will not scream. I think of the lion, gorged in the woods. His meat, until now, has never been heart. In the woods rise weeds, a messy world of unseparated things. Raptors above us. Big cats mewl. Mounds of apes wake amazed, no cages.

## The Bladder

The man who is told he will lose his bladder calls his bladder "The Haunted Lake." Like a story built from other stories, someday a new organ will be made from other body parts. I imagine what those parts will be: elastic like the wrist, thin like the skin where the cheek meets the tragus of the ear. For now, a kind of mushroom has begun to grow along the inner lining of his bladder. Doctors scrape the lining; but then, the mushrooms again. You would have to swim into that lake, he says, not breathe for days, to kill its monster. That's how he talks. That's the only way.

## The Crown of Light at Assisi

> *"We are looking for what is looking."*
> —attributed to Francis of Assisi

San Damiano, I'm told, has been repaired, a marvel at the bottom of the hill. Against the bicep width of olive trunk I watched a blade of grass a school of snails were climbing. Their footfalls were lighter than air. The blade hardly bent at their weight. I'm a blade of grass, a waving spine. The hollow brain up at the top. The heart is alive, in tow.

\*

At the Hermitage one half butterfly, half bee lands on my rain-wet journal, the words, "too beautiful to ever die." I've made a list: first, your acts of kindness, then the parents you forgave, then the eyes you healed, the ears, then leprosies, then how you learned to speak with birds, calling them to hear you teach them nothing, assuring them with gestures of the hand.

\*

On her sarcophagus, Calvetta's head is flanked on one side by a pine cone; on the other by a robin. Beautiful things are coming to term and some will not survive, the servants of the words lament. I am a servant of that wisdom, and I know what they mean. Calvetta lived her twenty years twenty centuries ago. A pine cone is much lighter than the body. A robin is much lighter than the body. These solutions don't console me.

\*

Your limestone pillow is shined by faces: those who slept here after you did. Your cave was cut out by a hand-held pick. I always want proof, I want to take a picture, I want to say things with authority. The lens doesn't care what I want. It will settle on what's here. Rain, the slime and green of living stone, and an image enters in. Whatever you desired in your authoring, the stone bed seems to say, rest here.

### Events Surrounding my Supposed Birth

Time kept passing and I wasn't getting born. My parents called and called for me. They made me a room, erected a tiny straw bed. Athens fell and shattered into bits, then Rome took a broom to the world. It was passing before I could open my eyes. My eyelids still so thin I could see apparitions, figures moving just behind that scrim. Breughel the Elder lifted his brush—tilting his horny, drunk dancers. At that point the day and the night slammed together. Which locked me in their forceps hold.

## The Pancreas

The pancreas lies with its head tucked in the duodenum, upside down, the tail stretched over it, an animal curled in on itself. In the preserve jar of the belly, it sleeps like a strange, medieval remedy. When we sleep, Anicka, the pancreas secretes its life, reverting tonight's *toutlerre* into Germanic syllables again: *cake, meat, grass, blood*. All of this healing is out of our hands. I turn to you, completely unconscious. Completely unconscious, you turn to me.

Sleepwalking

As I reveal myself to the world, the world will be revealed to me. My father used to sleepwalk, hammering invisible nails into the walls of the house. Then his invisible hammer would land on his thumb. He held the skin. It beat with pain. To wake him up, I'd have to learn to speak in signs, practice the agony's grammar. I'd gently take the hammer from his hands. Waking he would see there was no hammer, no nail. No thumb. No skin. No sleeping. No waking. No need of saving.

## The Unicorn in Modern Memory

The unicorn was just a thin rhinoceros, authorities are saying now. But I don't believe it. The rhino is covered by plates like hard plaque, but the unicorn, I once heard, was the most sought after prey, always fleeing through the woods of our primeval memory. How does one resolve this contradiction? I believe my grandmother wanted to tell me. This was as she rose to leave the house in the middle of the night. And with no warning in particular, her singing voice transformed into an Alzheimer's sigh.

## The Sleepers

I am running under trees and clouds, this is how I see my life. Sometimes I touch your collarbone along the fissure, an old accident. Two kilometers from Krasna, we sleep like that, in your dead grandmother's bed, my hand resting softly on your once broken shoulder. It is the room your mother made for us. Your parents, too, step into their massive wooden beds. Then moon pours through the windows on our bones. Gardenias painted on the walls. Death's white calmness. Oh, it is you, my body keeps seeming to say to your body. In a room that has filled up with sheep.

## In Translation: Woe-Mood

A word in this language, *vemod*, woe-mood, has no direct English translation. Anicka is describing her father's last breath—*huhp*, she says, breathing in deeply. "He was enveloped in our *vemod*," she says. A writing desk stands in the background, inert, its oak slab thrust out like a tongue. It has a blotter, some writing still depressed in it. Anicka bears a vague resemblance to the woman in the photograph in 1920. I keep looking at the photograph, feeling very sad, then back at her again.

## Max Jacob's Prayer List at Drancy

"I've forgotten no one in my continuous prayers," the French prose poet Max Jacob wrote the Abbot upon his reassignment at Drancy. The Gestapo had not heard of his conversion, would not have understood his strange poems anyway. There exist two sheets of paper covered with names, from Picasso to Jean Cocteau and others, too, artists who would not have wanted or asked for his prayers. Of course, grace is not dependent on belief: it visits independent of our wishes or our need. The author of the prayer was in the gravest danger but I've yet to find his name on these lists. The writing at the end grows tiny. Some names are just a squiggle, a mustache.

## "May I See What You Are"

I was waiting for what stirred inside the reeds to stir again, when I asked, *May I see what you are,* and quieted my life, felt my heart clank like a cup inside, up and down the cell bars of the ribs. But nothing moved. I thought about the day reprieves won't come, despite my having other plans, how I might beg but I will lose myself, lose you, and then I felt the question slipping from me. A wave smashed up against the shore. But it was not a shore, not a wave, not really. It didn't matter already. I wasn't looking when the stork began to flush and—*now see what I am*—open its colossal wings.

# Fat

Save everything, throw away nothing, my people taught me, and that's why my home is all mismatching silver, all mirrors and discordant furniture. This TV used to be my grandmother's. It's still warming up, tuned to the channel with cowboy shows playing. On the radio clock it is three a.m. Her fattening spirit gets up in the dark, does its chores in the dark to her shows. Today it's Tex Ritter. *Goodbye, my little Cherokee,* he sings to my grandmother, who bows as she tips down her percolator.

## Gender Study

I came down with a deadly flu and soaked through all our shirts, until we had none left, so Anicka lifted off her summer dress, she lowered it over her body. It was her mother's dress, too big for her anyway. Her mother had died that year. I lay there freezing, sweating, a dead woman's dress for my shirt. Anicka poured the wash into the tub. I really want to live, I prayed, as if I knew how. And I was heard. Or I heard "it." The sound of shirts, swishing, circled her hands, a nest of sexless angels.

# The Most Natural Thing

The woman cracked a walnut into halves and filled the halves with wax. A birthday candle in each one, she set the halves afloat, in milk. Gently she lifted the spine of the carp: it rose from the flesh in one sweeping motion. The carp lay on the table an unbuttoned sleeve. They ate the carp. The candles fizzled down. On the table was a watch, a white handkerchief. On the floor lay a doll, the eyes half opened, like hers, its painted eyebrows slightly raised.

## Removal

To feel each branching outward part. I do not feel each part, though I have prayed to hear the small breath of my cells at Wet Mountain. The aspen grove sends messages in leaf-code to its heart, a clutch of roots. Mildew zones out in the provinces. Burn up, burn up, the yellow aspen says, which is another way of saying remember who you are, as you move in your beautiful, arched upward body, believing yourself to be your own kingdom, believing yourself to be only yourself, instead of the land.

From: *ANOTHER CITY* (2018)

## City of Birth

The wound rips open. You feel the welt of being separate, its hospital lights. Then you know you have arrived. It is to be one body, held in the palm of the doctor's hand. It is the gash of being seen. Now for the rest of your life you are trying to be born through a wound. By some slip, or by a move more desperate, you've burned a purple shadow on your body. But death is not the subject of our portrait. It is the knowing you are seen. It is the lighting of one's light. It is to take a body, aware that you are not the body.

## Carp

Because it has fed
on the bottoms of rivers, and got fat,
we buy the carp at Christmastime.
It bends in its U in the porcelain tub.

With rolled-up sleeves my father
lifts the carp, winds a white rag
round its eyes. He uses the hammer
to quiet the suck of its mouth,
the tail's denials, its thumping.

The carp was introduced in Western water
seven hundred years ago. But it came
from farther east: its body continually
revising itself. With one slice down the side
he opens it, his awful Bible.

## Chance

On the train to Copenhagen I see Christina again. It's still the 1980s. I'm still a student of logistics with my backpack full of texts. Christina's hoping she will find some work at the casinos. One summer in the white apartment in Copenhagen, I shared a bed with her and her lover, Jens. I'd pretend to sleep while they fucked quietly. We would all lie in the bed the next day smoking King cigarettes. I am holding a cigarette and Christina is holding a cigarette. It's the moment chance has clasped into a quick and easy knot. We see in the other what it would have been like. To meet her like this: not *what* but *how* were the chances; how blurrily they course like trees; and at the doors of our separate compartments we are sliding shut the locks. It's still the 1980s. I'm still so good, I'm still stupid with my long hair and embarrassing excuses. I have a narrow bunk that pulls out like a drawer.

## Q: In What City Does Your Mother Live

In which she wears the jeweled shell
sometimes called the scarab beetle
who colors its walled castle bloody.
She wears the scarab Monday
when she drinks back fat white pills.
She wears it Tuesday when she falls.
She wears the scarab Wednesday
with the shredded lips that pray
to only swallow, turning blue. Thursday
with the angry morphine. She will try
to talk again on Friday, not to be asleep.
Saturday they wash with oil and soap.
For all that, Sunday is the law. Sunday
in her castle, folded wings and walls.

## Ardor

My place was under the table.
I remained there like a muffled lamp.
Seated above me, along my table-sky,
my parents and their good friends
laughed so hard my planets shook.

They struck their matches, tiny plosives.
Against the table-sky they slammed
their fists. One man was very drunk.
He fell like he'd been pushed. His eyes
met mine at my place under the table.

My small green soldiers, too,
would sometimes lose their dignity.
It was a quality I loved about them.
They all had in common an absolute
sureness, their ardor to die.

Preservation

The Little Boy Blue on the wall at ease
in his leggings, hips sashayed. The Pink Girl
shadowed by her measly parasol. The figures
never aging, man on his horse, her pearl
jawline round and bursting with a toothache,
in agony, her horse-eyes, their logic
human, looking at my looking back at you.
Because I was the only one left in the room.
Because I will be always. Because I will be
always. Because you suddenly let go of time.

## The Liquid R

It was a language of white hills, red brick towns.
An alley was a comma in the agony's grammar.

It was the old one tied against a chair, madness
swelling like a thought too big for her head,

and each death was a period. The mortician a stain,
a drop of ink in his black suit, before a page-white mausoleum.

It was a language of yeast soup, snowy hills, towns
called Beauty and Cold, where the names of things

had some corresponding order, beauty always going
cold, always losing itself to something permanent.

There was carp at the fishmonger, butcher paper
where the meat was weighed. Time at the clockmaker's shop.

There were syntactical surprises: the headmaster
turned janitor inside of a day, the ambassador

seen on the subway in tattered clothes, the president
dressed as prisoner, delivering his acceptance speech,

the secret police as tourists on their own beat.
But mostly it was a language one used when speaking

in a whisper, rolling the R, practicing the R
in your mouth until it dropped from the palate

to the tongue as from the pocket of God, and hung there
momentarily in its shiny majesty, a sound much older

than the language that spent it, that offered it from one mouth
to another.

# Hymn

We are somewhere in a story, a certain hymn begins.

It is the night the lights have failed.

My mother reclines
on the couch, the candles all around her.

My father hunches over the fuse box.

We are somewhere in a story, the hymn goes on.

It is the story in which each of us is making up a story.

And we search for each other: we hold the candles out,
but only light our own faces.

We are somewhere in a story,
the hymn repeats.

It is the last verse no one ever seems to know.
It is the one we mouth the words to, watching

other mouths mouth words, in the dark
church of memory.

## My Town

Sometimes my town is deserted. The streets are dark except for a luminous bookstore window. Inside is a poet I loved in my early days. Sometimes she's talking to a younger version of herself, and they're sipping wine in unison. Sometimes I'm lost in my town, and it's raining, and I can only speak Czech.

Sometimes I'm at my mansion on the outskirts. There's a soccer field, the sun is setting over it. My guests have bled out onto the lawns. Sometimes my parents are coming down the grand staircase still dressed in their coats for winter. Hello, my father says. Hello, my mother says, in much the same way.

Sometimes I'm walking toward my town, along a giant wall, and below the wall is a river, and across the river is another place, a city of the dead, and it reminds me of the Tuileries. I know I have a choice to go there or keep walking to my town, which I always do, which I have done so far, with its spires and bars, its windows with motionless skeleton faces.

## Letter from Rock Creek

*For Mary Oliver*

I want to ask you what that clicking sound
    is for, rising out of Rock
Creek Park, below my little room; but even you
    can't help me pin that down—so many miles

from here, where you are tucked in bed, your
    little room, your neck and chin concealed by the bark
of a burnt sienna scarf;
    so I leave it

as it is, our mood music, and I remember
    shore-days in the Provincetown house,
reading in Hopkins *Send my roots rain,*
    or anything by Keats, who was

drowned in his ceiling made of flowers,
    while this click in the background
persists, not cricket, some smallest-
    insect-on-record, small enough to be

a gnat's pilot, small like a certain quality
    you have courted in your poems, how you squint
and bend down to things, how you do not disturb
    their place, how this characteristic expands

in my mind exponentially as the objects
    themselves grow tinier: the closed hood
of the mushroom's umbrella at night,
    or the clam, an Osiris, locked in its bivalves,

which made a nice supper—how the God
    appears altered, *altared,* each time you look—even the
scrape of one wing against the other's
    leathery file, to stridulate, to make a click that carries

in mathematical waves, while this singer, untroubled
    by itself, goes on fine without an advocate, a name.

## Calling Horses

She calls our horses back through dark,
calls out of trees and land the running horses,
calls horses wild with their own thinking,
corral a cloud of dirt and tantrum kick.

It is her angriest voice, the hardness
like the voices of the gods through canyons.
It is knowing what is sent will be returned.
It is this voice in her I've never understood
but horses do what she expects of them, they come

to her loud clapping. They come because she asks.
She calls our horses back through dark
until the last, the penitent, who bends
so she can run the metal comb along the belly,
to clear the froth of white, protective sweat.

## "An Apartment in the City of Death"

*After a line by Kabir, translated by Robert Bly*

When I died
I moved into this empty

room. I thought
about who stayed here

before me: their hard
faces from the nineteenth

century, the wan
cheekbones, the true

God they believed, the
body a

lackluster horse.
not so much as

a single white candlestick
remains of them.

Not a flayed broom,
not one matchbook, not

a wood umbrella
camouflaged in shadow.

Soon, like they did,
I'll have stayed on so long

I'll be forced to die
all over

again. Then I'll huff off
to another city, smaller

room, away from here.

# Wave

Lincoln, leaving Springfield, 1861,
    boards a train with a salute: but it is weak.
To correct it, he slides his hand away
    from his face as if waving, as if brushing
the snows of childhood from his eyes.

The train is coming east. In the window
    Lincoln watches his face. You'll grow old
the moment you arrive, he says to this face.
    But you will never reach great age. The train
speeds like the cortical pressure wave

in the left lateral sinus, say, a bullet
    in the skull. Then he will have his salute.
Then they will love him. Then eternity will slow, fall
    like snow. Then the treaty with huge silence
which he, his face exhausted, must sign.

## A Young Man's Copybook: 1861–1864

*Conscription, September 1861*

By train we come to Philadelphia,
conductors patrolling

for drunkenness, illness, the mad.
We are no drunks. We are not ill.

We believe with our right minds, we say.
Come, they say, and we are greeted by steam, horse breath,

curt personnel, small cards that bear the family name.
From as far as Chester County, to the fortresses

of Quaker villages, we come to affix
to the rest of our days this

service: submission
to rank, by signature.


\*


When we were little children, we would write
as children do, with pencil tips. We wrote

our stories in great loops, each practiced letter
scaled to the size of the thumb.

From my shoulder Jacob read out words
and I pressed down the words. The words

were my pressed flowers, the words
would flatten as flowers do. The pencil left

light markings, easily erased, like everything
I touched back then. I did no harm

with words. But outstretched like a stinger
in my father's fist would be the Cornwall pen:

that was my first weapon,
unalterable its strokes.

\*

Where is he now, my Jacob
who pressed flowers in the pages of my copybook,

whom I reproached for being delicate.
Where am I now, who drew broad signs, flags, eagles

toting banners in their grip.
Where is the train that rocked me out of sleep

and Jacob at the window, hollering.
The sun almost up. Philadelphia: a field of smoke,

horse breath, curt
personnel, their tents and protestant, plain desks.

I have never seen the young more joyous in the world,
dressed that morning by our mothers.

\*

*When Walt Whitman Came
to Stone General Hospital, April 1864*

We mewled to him
    More peaches
and a bowl of cream

and called him Father
    Walt, and he then gave
a nickel when he had

a nickel, and he then fed
    a strawberry, its hairs
like the tongue of a cat

on my tongue
    on days I would ask,
Did you bring me

the *Iliad*? And Walt sang,
    Rage be now your song
in a voice that caught

and flung against the high-
    ceilinged warehouse
and its walls, falsetto

unlike the sergeant
    but as detached as news.
The wheels of carriages

outside bore mounds of us
    away, arms, legs, hands,
more parts of us cut out

into something heavy
    for the long straight

roads where they would burn.
Walt Whitman's
    voice was curvy,
full of ruts.

He kissed us on the
    forehead, then on the lips,
then on the cheek.

\*

*After Charges of Desertion, June 1864*

I saw my river, one kid

stood fishing there,
not even waving

to a passing man
in uniform. My long

coat brushed
the ground, I was taller,

in my boots,
maybe my feet

weren't touching, my beard
the only weight,

like leader fishing line,
my hair like tippet,

and that's
my story, that's when

the cough discharged,
the sad, black

blood—exit ink.


\*


On record I'm a cad, the object of a bounty, rogue escaper from the rough.

My lawyer like a doting mamma, walked to and fro with his black bags, between the offices on Small Street.

But the word had dried already.
Think of my face:

A face the witness reconstructs.
A face that takes its leave.

## Comet

Lincoln is sent back to Springfield, the third of May, the victim of bad embalming. Nearly three weeks have passed. His face takes on a fast collapsing, melted gaze. If there were some way he could see what he's become, grotesque, green Jesus of the hour, returning dead to the dead he left here, including one son, he would turn away his head. He would signal for the train to keep traveling. He would let the towns blaze past him, the cities of the living, people pointing with their hands, this death a tail of ice.

BEATIFICATION

The only soul
who beatifies itself

is the lightning bug
of America

also called Firefly
also called:

Half-in-love-
with-dusty-death

also called
Slant-of-light

also known as
Hobo-who-believes-

he's-Jesus
and You-

oh-my-soul
greased with luciferase

my consort
arriving on fire

as *Lampyridae*
flash dactylic

like apple tree—
like crucifix—

like undertow—
you are the one

lit from inside
as you venerate your life

to children
and I chased you

through darkness
my hands thrust

in front of me
as I sealed shut

my fist
and squeezed—

## "Marie Curie's Century Old Radioactive Notebook Still Requires Lead Box"

A book that casts its own light
and a hundred years since you,
who lived a spell in the tick
of its lamp, stood from your chair.

The book is closed and finished.
But the box must be lit from inside,
so I can see you thumb another
page, each new page brightening.

If I mentally turn on the lamp,
if I were to open the lead-vested
box: maybe I would find you there,
your gaze like a photograph seared

into the page. You finished this book.
You will not return to it. Also
you must stay here, obsession being
what scorches but does not burn out.

Lovesickness

The octopus loved her naturalist so deeply, soon the giant, ink-filled head remained permanently flat on her shoulders, looking upward from the aquarium as the other gazed down into it. Then an egg the size of a grain of rice fell from the octopus. Distance is sometimes confused for love. I've begun feel so far from myself, I want to have a child.

## X, & Axe

From down this creek
        came men on flatbeds riding
on the wide green world
        as it was then.

There was a team of nodding
        broken horses,
there was a team
        of men I never saw before

who broke the old barn
        into its packet-parts,
board and beam and windowpane,
        hutch and doorframe,

who flattened down
        the imperfections
to a chart of transits,
        an equation for which $x$

would be the labor of their hands.
        Then rode backward
on the flatbed facing
        where the barn was razed:

our hands raised waving
        as they left. They have gone
on forty years, riding
        backward on the flatbed

the barn gone too
        the meadow gone
all gone downcreek
        although I cannot say

how it was they took it
>	with them, made it small enough
to carry through the slit
>	of twilight,

as through the two bars
>	of an equals sign they disappeared
between the darkness
>	and the land.

## Embarrassment

En route to California, after crossing snowy Monarch Pass, I'd pull into a bar on Highway 50 called the Bear Claw. At his table my dead father sat in the green sleeveless jacket with orange on the inside. Or now and then the jacket was reversed, depending on whether he was hunting me or hiding.

Where have you been, I asked him, and he told me of the cities he had visited in death: Cherbourg, France, where there was a disappointing fistfight, and the streets of Manila, where he thought his murderer had been following him, but it was only himself as a young man, holding a pair of lost glasses in hand. In Port-au-Prince he had been a child living off crisp fish he ate in tiny bites, cooked over a barrel by the sea. He had been in my mother's house many times, unable to fix his contraptions as one by one they failed her.

My father was a man always crouched in a pose against embarrassment, which I inherited. So I understood. That's why I never reached California, and I would turn around each time, risking my life all over again on Monarch Pass.

## The Leatherback

It is dying, this heaviest of turtles. So magnetized to earth, great is its labor to be itself being, to move with sliding steps the brown flippers. Now it rests in the no-man's-land of dry sand, having lost its way like my father did, on his path back to bed, when he fell and I could not lift him. The dying are always the heaviest, until they reach the wave.

## The Sibilant

We had the Latin of the waves at night.
We had the vernacular of tears.
We had the alternate ending, plan B,
in which we stayed together. We had
plan A, in which we would part.

We had the letters I have burned,
in which you spoke of our past life
as married, in a forest, on bicycles,
the trees angry seraphim, and darkness
coming. We had this now, not that.

We had that once, now this.
The sun was neither rising nor setting.
Our kisses plosives. The sex, the one time,
is sibilant: *shh*, before you cross the room
in a nightgown, the knock at the door.

## A Blue Dish

My mother lives alone the first six months
without my father. She keeps things as they are.
The absences are still high up: top three inches
of the bedroom door threshold; fog of an unshined
transom; the coffee tone of dusk in porticos.

When she is gone, absence will sink down
and even fill the square blue dish
at the center of the kitchen table. It is the blue
of my father's anchor tattoo, faded to a powder;
the color of a needle's bruise below the crepe.

The dish was passed down from my father's line.
It came to this house, tattooed on its architecture.
She lives alone with it. Then the dish is mine,
its absences like apple, pear, blue color of a fall
with Icarus, soft night, little cutout stars.

## The Little Stairs of Z

The puffs of rising Zzs above my head,
I am about to fall asleep, to climb
them well beyond the borders
of my cartoon cloud, when I hear
the first horse huff and stamp its foot.

It is the palamino, Sailor Boy,
dead for twenty years. Then not only horses
but the snails I met in Assisi, so small they climb
the blades of grass. Then the boxer
I carried up steps all her life,

the front right leg never healing.
*What is the sun you've made of yourself*
she asks, and all the animals stand waiting.
With the rile of the calves brought to the slaughterhouses
of childhood. With the monkeyish cat, leukocytes
amok like mice.

## My Father's Hours

I went searching for a clue
of some collaboration

between the two
who ruled that house

with its discouragements
for a glance or the Morse

of clicking silverware
as on the late-shift nights

over the chair he hung
his heavy green coat

and then his hard hat
by its strap of white plastic

and like a man
in an elevator falling

he would stand frozen
the work still loud in his body

what was the story he told himself
coming home on these evenings

was his life
when I met him at the door

in my pajamas of men on motorcycles
all of them helmeted impassive

doing wheelies in the air
Now up the wooden hill he said

and he pointed his finger
at nothing

## My Carnation

In the city I'm traveling to,
awnings billow up in wind and light.
Winter is early. We are surprised
we are surprised. The waiters
in their tiny jackets pull their jackets

close against the sudden cold.
In the city I'm traveling to, I arrive
on the train, its only passenger.
A man in black clothes helps me down.
A constable is twirling his baton.

A servant bears my latched-up trunk,
but ruefully, ruefully. He is gone.
A certain old woman is waiting to sell me
my carnation: to offer it with one hand,
to cover her teeth with the other.

## Magic

In the padlocked trunk before they dropped him
in the river, Houdini was said to foresee
his mother's death. Stuck in his box, at the end
of a chain, he felt the death, its approach,
her worry growing smaller at the eyes as she

removed herself from herself, her body shrunken
to the size of a keyhole. I believe that grief
can travel distances like that. My mother's
cough would wake me up at night, two hundred
miles away. That was a year ago, before she

got too small. She drowned in a cloud
of bright white baby hair. She lay on the bed
as if on a board, the last I saw her, still and calm.
Then truly as if a lever were pulled, she tipped
backwards, out of view.

## "Every Angel Is Terrifying"

There was the time     one of the younger deer
stepped into the hedges at the house
that we called Homewood     and through an open window
he lowered the shale colored muscular shoulders
his eyes met my eyes     and pushed     partway through

I thought it was to see who was alive in here
or to offer some encouragement     with his aware
impassive face     may I stay heavy on this mind
I found myself requesting     may part of me remain
behind these eyes     but it did not     the herd continued

down their unmown road and the deer     at the window
broke his gaze and turned     and followed them
This was the start of some new work for me
it was the fall
I had been trying to untangle all my questions     I wished

that I was not myself     I never saw the angel after that
time passed     nor did the herd return
I went back to what I had been doing all along
except that I could feel   a certain focus   the concentration
of a being     standing watching     what I am

## Empire, Discourse

When he was old my father traveled back to Rome
though forty years had passed. With my mother
he sipped red wine out in the sun along the via
Appia, when he thought he saw me wave at him
from somewhere up ahead and turn away. It wasn't
me, I was in another city, I'd tell him after that but
for the remainder of my father's life he would insist
on this story, until I started to imagine how far I'd be
by now, that road a continuous grave, the broken
open tombs and catacombs, the turreted Aurelian
Walls, my father always coming to the end by saying
You must have had some place to get to so I let you go.

# On Three

(New Poems)

# Composition for Three Voices: a Tenement in Moravia

*First Flat: Irena's Voice*

We have a word that's very difficult. Its parts skip backward on the tongue. A word as much to swallow as to say. And when you say it, you will be one of us. *Ch-te-ver-tek*. English: Thursday. *Čtvrtek*. But you must carve it, like tough meat, into parts. Why am I alive? During war (this is difficult to say) men from another city, it was Havirov, called on my mother every Thursday. Cakes, milk, bread, sometimes a bit of meat or butter, they paid her for their privileges. *Čtvrtek* was the hardest word, hardest day. I am alive because I ate the whole meal every Thursday.


*Second Flat: Ferda's Voice*

Over the town the stacks blew a cape made of ashes. Magic shows rely on simple faith. A man cannot be cut in two, sit up and try to walk away. A woman can't just disappear. A tongue cannot be shredded cloth, pulled out of the mouth. So beliefs instruct. The ride into Poland had many stops. They stopped in this town. They stopped over there and others waved from the platform. They asked for some to step forward. They took our hands sometimes and helped us on the train. They asked us little questions on our hopes and destinations. We believed in the trick and stepped into their boxes with the slots where the knives go in.

*Third Flat: Pavel's Voice*

The Dead of Winter, was the part I played. It was a small role and I never spoke. Sometime in March in 1945 my boots were stolen. With feet as cold as iron I stood sweeping snow from the tent in the last hours of the world. Where am I, where am I going, I thought, the snows of wartime passing over my head. If I keep moving, I'll live, so I will not bequeath my iron feet to anyone, therefore I have no children, no wife, no flesh to pour this heaviness into. I am still that shoeless man standing upright with his broom, brimmed with ire. But I am also myself, a softer person. The shoeless man and I are floating on a stage. We lower the broom on each side, and row, through snow, until now.

## Hieronymous Bosch's Self Portrait in Hell

On the misunderstood third panel
Bosch's face turns and looks back

on what has become of his body:
he is merely amused, a smile

beginning to match the recognition
that he has become somewhat porcine,

though the legs of this strange pig
soon morph into branches of a white

tree. The pig's backside is shattered
like an egg, cracked open to reveal

three demons sitting at a long table
drinking from a pitcher that now rests

in the relaxed grip of the middle one.
They seem to be having an OK time.

They are naked and explaining them-
selves. Every detail reveals another

ho-hum routine: they sit along a green
bench, or rather, it is a kind of alligator

creature. On Bosch's head a stone
disc presses down like a hat, one he

sports tilted, with panache. At the brim
a few nude souls are given their own

not so much a torturer as personal
entertainer, so in promenade they

march in circles to keep Hell spinning
for as long as they can, which is for-

ever, while the Thing with the face
of a hummingbird, delighted by his station,

keeps time by thrusting upward his baton.

# 222 West Twenty-Third Street

Rage will have to learn gentleness.
It will not be for the light, or against it.
My father wouldn't leave us when he died,
getting up and blowing out our candles,

blasting the ballasts of halogen
in his former house. He wanted to unset
the sun along the trees where it would flatten.
My mother on the other hand would fight

to never look again straight into mirrors,
and passed the big one in the upper hall
many times without acknowledging

her eggshell hands, the crumpled hairs,
in her attitude that none of this was real,
but staged for someone's weird, kind-hearted laughing.

## Composition for the Faith of Clifford Brown

> *Had Goodman Brown fallen asleep in the forest*
> *and merely dreamed a wild dream...?"*
> —Hawthorne, *Young Goodman Brown*

On June 25, 1956
   it is a hard bop, Max
Roach on drums,

that brings you up
   to Philadelphia,
it's reported, to Music

City, I have heard tell,
   to serenade a wall
of cigarette smoke

stone sober,
   with tinkling glass
and ashtrays falling

down slow motion,
   your second to last night
alive. There is much

to get wrong about
   this story, like any
story often riffed,

how it was not,
   on the following night,
your wife but Richie

Powell's who did
   the driving and the rain
I once believed was pouring

on the empty PA turnpike
   was falling instead
on a town called New Bedford

near Pittsburgh, as your party
   passed through dead
tired. I can't know

if you fell, in slow motion,
   asleep in the passenger seat,
because you wanted

to relax your hands.
   I can't know if you wanted
to lay your head

against your Buick's
   thick window, and sleep
to the sound of syn-

copated raindrops
   spattering in flutes
across the glass,

or even if you intended
   with the faith of twenty-
five-year-olds,

to wake up fresh;
   still famous; only halfway
through a hard storm;

still Clifford; still full
   of wild gifts; at rest
and in the city of Chicago.

# The Dice Cup

I believe that the one carrying eggs, the one who walks along the Loire, has been carrying the eggs for six hundred years. I believe she's the sister of St. Joan of Arc, who crawled on her knees in the church to take up her sword. I have followed the prints of Joan's knees in the church. I have lashed myself for being weak, which is disquiet. I have lashed myself for being sullen, which is complaint. I believe that Joan's sister was constantly dropping the eggs. I believe that she blamed herself harshly, wholeheartedly. As she bent down to pick one up, more eggs fell out of her apron. Stupid, stupid. But they had not broken.

## Pearl Street

The man I saw on Pearl Street in Boulder was naked except for a loincloth. He stepped into a small glass box on the street, and by some process unhinged and unhooked his arms and legs from their sockets. He fell into the box and looked out at us. That was enough for a show, I remember myself thinking. This is actually the whole show.

\*

The carried quality of a poem: that it has come from far away, that it is true. The feeling comes, from the first pages, that one is reading the murals of a cave wall. Flickering light. Something frightening, something wondrous, told with attention, which is where the love comes in.

\*

Every argument ever made could be countered with the true statement, but there's more to it than that.

\*

The world has always been full of stubborn children who throw away their toys and prefer to play with the boxes.

\*

The city in winter an undeveloped Polaroid. Nothing but snow and black sky, nothing moving on Cathedral Avenue. And the buck stepped calmly into the streetlight.

\*

Vision is impossible to maintain for very long, before the framework collapses again. The most haunting images are brief.

\*

The photographer has elbowed in on something that is only halfway through. My grandfather is at work on the top of a man's head. The man is just as old as he, looking into the mirror, at us, and at the man with the camera, who stands behind them. They are both the age that I am now. I know that shop by heart – the small drawer where he kept packets of razor blades and bazooka gum; the rack of coats and hats against the back wall; the washroom in the closet to the right; the mirror with its proscenium view of everything, everyone, so that by looking straight ahead you can also look around; the white ashcan with the foot-pedal that flipped the lid; my own white hair is inside.

\*

Most of us are not Osip Mandelstam. Most of us merely have to die to our embarrassment. To reveal ourselves as we are without hesitation or prettification.

\*

A metaphor begins in dissonance and ends in harmony.

\*

Sometimes there is a point where you are no longer the boat floating on the water, subject to its rising and falling, but you become the water.

\*

Write about nothing. Nothing is more vast than nothing.

\*

If you hang on to your wish to play Oedipus the Golden Child, you've got to play Agony, too.

\*

The way certain architecture uses spaciousness to quiet one part of the mind, or humble its rambling complaints, while in another part of the body, we'll call that the imagination, a wideness, a with-ness, is possible.

\*

I started writing poems to inflate my life. Then poetry came along as a pin to pop it.

\*

St. Benoit-sur-Loire, the thousand-year old church, the knee-molded, shoe-kneaded floors as if on a wave that had gone suddenly still.

\*

Tiresius interpreted the configurations of birds. Dante and Moses climbed mountains. It's the outsiders and exiles—and the dying—who perceive from their "sad height" what we cannot.

\*

The prayer cards and Bible and the statues of saints on my mother's side of that bed. On my father's side, the big book with its diagrams of our universe, the Andromeda galaxy and the Milky Way; my mother's side with her chipped Saint Jude (patron saint of Lost Causes) and novenas for the deathly ill. On both sides of the bed were a kind of magic—science and words could, through meticulous trial and error, embody the vast richness of history and time; the Bible and prayer cards and the magic incantations were outside of time and used language in a purely lyrical way—to escape itself.

\*

Louisa Amato, who owned the Grolier Book Shop back then, approached me where I waited at the steps of her store, dressed in my blue suit, a half an hour before she was to open. "Are you a poet or a sales representative," she asked. It was a pretty good question, and still is.

\*

Moving ourselves around won't bring it any closer. Nor would willful standing still. Just acknowledge that force, Dante suggests, and you move beyond even faith. To simply know it exists is to surrender to it.

\*

He was doomed to look down at the page when describing the sky.

\*

"Without contraries is no progression," wrote William Blake in *The Marriage of Heaven and Hell*. I almost tattooed that on my arm, but I was of two minds about it.

\*

So many myths of origin begin with a togetherness that chose to be divided. In those stories, the point is not to acquire anything but to remember who you are.

\*

Two conditions often set the stage for good poetry. One is imposed silence; the other is lack of paper. Prison poems carry an urgency and an *economy* that most of ours do not.

\*

The more intense our love, the more we are reminded of the boundaries of our bodies. Love is freedom and love is a prison. The genius of love is its incomprehensible dissonance.

\*

Assisi: Below the cathedral is the unearthed tomb of the man Francis. It's just a vessel holding, fittingly, nothing.

\*

The language of cathedrals is the tongue of Meister Eckhart, of Rumi and Kabir, of the countless other mystics whose subject is the silence of God.

\*

Jorge Luis Borges once said to a crowded lecture hall at Harvard University that "a word is a dead metaphor," and with that he summed up all our troubles as writers.

\*

That the closer you look at a thing the farther away it retreats; how it becomes porous, then almost invisible, then was never there.

# Three Close Readings in a Darkening Time

1. *Reading* Heart of Darkness *in the 21st Century*

The English are swatting at horseflies
in their Tudor-shaped huts
somewhere on a giant river of lies,
and the river smacks me in the face

as I open up the book again. Again Kurtz
in his pleats lifts a porcelain cup at table
and grunts. He's sat so long in my cabinets,
shoved between the King James Bible

and the Donne, he's barely awake: He has a tiny
golden chair; a face like an overstuffed purse.
He's going to patiently watch this,

and take his small sips, until he shows me
something horrible again, where brutality mills
the heart into the smallest particles.

2. *Reading* The Divine Comedy *Backwards in Ravenna*

Nothing changed in his tomb now visited by no one
on a street where Byron also took a room
I had followed him like an inspector come from Florence
with its Guelph flags he'd still recognize above the Arno
the Paradise to which he could not return the fish smell of leather
and his cordoned off bedroom and the lost books

Then to Siena by the frayed stained tablecloths and black soup at night
I descended the circular mountain of town facing screaming
antique racecars coming up against me a man waving
me off the road singing *Vai! Vai! Vai!* smoking a Galois

But in Ravenna was his Hell: my impoverished room a few million
liras a night and the shower doors cities of *mycelium*
the toilet Malebolge with huge flies whose names were all Geryon
as around that labyrinth of hot streets aggressive vendors
swam in their own lake of sweat their toys for children already
seven hundred this year year of medieval indecencies

After the stars he saw the source of light I ask who could be lost here
after the dome at San Vitale like the mouth of gold fillings
after its figure impaled on the altar on that mouth's bottom tooth
his death like walking backwards in a dark wood into the cypresses again

3. *Reading* Gilgamesh *Before Going to Sleep*

In some dreams it is possible to visit Uruk and to be its king
as I did sensing all along I was a bad king predisposed
to impatience and affronted by impertinence and I know now
what I really needed was a good friend who could teach me things

Then that happened as I fell asleep with my arm
on the barrel-chested dog prone to snoring and standing straight up
on the bed at night or barking at the snap of thunder or a neighbor slamming
his fist into a wall next door I have known all along I am my own bad friend

but we have killed the monster loneliness and though injured
with a bum leg and then the hips and then the kidneys failing
the dog kept showing me what I am not how I am not like her
not uncomplaining not joyful in a time of joy not undeterred by things unseen

not guarded in a time of danger and when she left I walked through oceans of
    myself
like Gilgamesh searching for a way to stay in pain forever
because I didn't know how else to honor what had died for me
—Yes I was wrong of course I was an idiot a king of human beings

and when I had the chance to live I was distracted anyway—
Then it was possible to see the rheumy eyed and coughing old
citizens of my city and to weep for what I should have known
that I was the rheumy eyed and coughing citizen dying which is the only way
                      to visit Uruk and to become its king

### Justice, Three Panels

THE TELEVISION LOST HORIZONTAL
exactly as the execution was performed.

The screen rippled upward making the work
of bearing witness difficult. It was many years

ago. One of the men was tied by his hands
and feet. His face was flying upward, upward.

The staggered glimpses of his exaggerated, blue eye.

\*

IN THE TALE OF THE FOOLISH POLICE CHIEF,
Husan al-Din must find the robber of the gold.

He gathers all the people of the khan and tosses
them in jail. But when a man confesses, those people

praise and bless the culprit for his goodness, and Husan
is called a brute. This is why they help the robber steal the money

back, and he escapes into the crowds of Alexandria.

\*

EVERY ACTION HAS A DESIGNATED
punishment before that action is erased.

My teacher of Geometry was a master of such formulae.
He had written all the theorems by himself.

He sat at his desk, his feet in the air. The answers
to the tests were locked inside the battered pencil drawer.

We started writing at his "word," aptly followed by our sucking
   in of breath.

## Pictures of my Family

My father's laughter in the open air
on an oiler deck in the sweat of Gibraltar
and the summer. My mother
dressed to spend the day indoors.

Some of these seem genuine.
But in some, the light is moon,
or the contrast is degraded, the pictures
too old. My grandfather wears

an oversized suit, as he walks somewhere
soaked in the rain. My great-grandfather
the ragman in a doorway, his horses
stamping behind him. In some of these

I find the glaze of small dabs, vague
corrections. My parents embracing.
Me, the eyes all scissored out
and pasted on again, a sort of ransom note.

# Only the Marvelous is Beautiful

*Acceleration*

By the time they knew the galaxies were accelerating, I was living in the small town with the Russian spires a hundred years in the past, spending my time at the Café Goethe, writing so fast in my notebooks I can't read a word of them now. Then Freud was just born in a place called Pribor, south of there, as Shor came up with his quantum algorithm to solve the modern sphinx riddle, involving the integer N and its prime factors. But I was already in the eighteenth century by then, and falling back quickly, until the town was just a field full of scythes and gleaners speaking a protolanguage too spare to understand, and I was as small as a neutrino in my serfdom, floating through grass and identical days.

*A Small Mirror*

I was mostly too weak to look up from my crib, at the small baby dresser, with the small baby blanket, and the small baby mirror. I didn't know what I'd become. The time before this time, when I had been old and big, I was broken at the hips. After a while, I could grip on the bars of my crib and bend at the sacrum, and straighten again. Of course I used none of these words. In the big world downstairs I saw the linked arms; then it was a knotted, angry mob. At first I thought the screen was another mirror. It got confusing. The confusion has lasted, to tell you the truth, though I don't speak of it much anymore.

*Late into the Night*

It was already over for America, but no one knew that yet. The wrinkled A-line dress and Victory suit hung from racks at The Charm Shop in my mother's town. Her sisters worked through high school, in the windowless room, blue detergents swimming in their eyes and blood. There were many turbans to launder and they worked late into the night. There were piles of overalls and red bandanas from the war years. The sisters dumped the turbans in a basket and carried them upstairs. The shop was empty. From the basket they lifted each one with two hands. Bikinis sold well, and sandals with peep-holes, and there must have been hundreds of pairs of saddle shoes, piled high, which they shined under the single bulb lamp in their faces, in perfect health in a time of growth.

*Buñuel*

No one speaks the name of Luis Buñuel. He prefers to be nameless among the crowds in the shadow of the Empire State Building. The Republic has fallen. The war is a giant gorilla climbing the right side of his brain, waving off ideas like small airplanes. Lorca is dead and is buried on a hill in Grenada—Buñuel, if anyone, can know such things—with a bullfighter and a schoolteacher. Lorca is himself, of course, and Dalí is the bullfighter, of course, and Buñuel is, of course, the schoolteacher; and each of them, in their own way, has gone underground. Dalí has died the death of popularity. Buñuel has chosen the slow death of silence. He will leave for Mexico by the end of the decade, but for now he sits in a shabby diner on Lexington Avenue, cutting with his knife and fork (he always uses two hands, for he will always be a European) through the sunny side yolk of an egg, which stares right back at him, not even flinching.

*A Movie Scene*

Elegantly I dance down to the patio. The crowd widens to make space for me. How welcomed one feels in a movie scene, how careful the other dancers are, how they know who is the star, how happy the women swinging in white dresses in the revolving doors. Everything pushes away in a lab in equal proportion; so many things that irritate, under the best conditions, produce a lasting beauty. But if this were really the Thirties, like the rest of my family I would be a ragman, I would know how to ride a horse and flatbed, how to read the look of irritation in the faces when they saw me coming, as they stepped out of the way, I would know many other things than the things that I know now.


*"Only the marvelous is beautiful"*
    —André Breton

When "marvelous" began to mean "splendid," sometime in the twenties, to be splendid was merely to glitter, from *splendidus* in the Latin. André Breton never used the word in English, I suppose for its association to the spleen. My mother was not a surrealist but she loved things that glittered, from the twenties, especially. Why should I weep, I ask you, over this pair of opera glasses she kept in her curio cabinet, the minuscule, gold binoculars I never once saw her lift to her face.

*Fin-de-Siècle*

In Renoir's great *Luncheon of the Boating Party,* in every direction on the canvas, forming an asterisk, the male gaze seeks a trajectory. The lines continue beyond the canvas, through the square of the gold frame, through the floor of the gallery, straight into mantle, each line like the ties securing a conquistador's galleon. The sand has always received such ropes, which are also sent up through the ceiling and through the west and east corridors, leading across Washington D.C. to the other great *The Boating Party*, Marie Cassatt's, which is on water, the boatman looking down along the line of the oar atop the gunwhale. But his sight gets caught in the green sail: as the woman, dressed in a full gown buttoned at the neck, gazes into the wind, toward something just out of focus, a century or more from now, so that I get the feeling of an imposition, my staring clearing indecent, how none of this has anything to do with me.

## Theory

> *Anonymous photograph of Einstein*
> *on a bike at Princeton in old age*

Old, milling, glad to meet you, *wunderbar*.
Draped with all the tangled, famous hair.

It is fall here on the first day of our classes.
There is the campus bell. The sweater

full of tiny thread-holes, moth wing
frail. I think he breathes by time alone,

dead holes, the inconvenient math,
the eerie, vague behavior of some types

of light. It's best to let the man get by, to step
aside. Do a little dance for him. His trajectory

already shaky as he steers, and seems to grip
the God weight, the tremor of the handlebars.

## My Solitude

I wanted to save you
but I kept arriving a moment too late,
to the smell of lavender and soap,
echo of wet powder, or what had been
the perfume of the guardians, the faint
vibrations of their hands.

### With Rilke in the Josefhov Quarter

*From a passage translated by Stephen Mitchell*

Now you are dead and I am in Josefov
and one hundred years have not gone by.
*The abundant rain of the heavy*

you might have called a universal gravity
to this quarter, this mess of a human city,
though you are dead. I am in Josefov

looking for you; and you were the Lev
whose monster mastered pain, born to play
(as the abundant rain does) the heavy

of Prague. In the crowded teeth of graves.
In Mucha, under soot. I know this melancholy.
But yours is long dead: in Josefov

you had to die to it, remove yourself, leave
for Paris. Or, even if you left this story
for the abundant, its ruin was still heavy

and it exhausted you, and this ravaged
your life. Then you would escape the body,
abandon its reign. The body was heavy.
Now it is dead. And I am in Josefov.

# Sonnet

> *You are that which is not.*
> Catherine of Siena

The stork has gone. Here is the nest.
It teeters on the station tower
like a satellite dish encircled in grass,
or tiny bits of hair, over and over,

or yarn around a pair of unseen hands.
Old transmissions have come to a hush.
The air is static whorl. The road wends.
I wonder at this *ghat*; this bull rush

basket; mouth-in-waiting for its tooth.
The stork was here. Here is the nest.
Praise the giving way, the taking wing.

Praise the singing bowl, after the song.
Praise who cast, from such delicate
bronze, an absence.

## Eulogy after a Convalescence

*For Fr. Hal*

The land in St. Benoit, where the Romans
had come to rest, was not the convalescence
he imagined. Now it was a moldered barn
of books in crates and nights of constant rain.
But he also had the unnamed road, the fence
for when he tired out, and he had its horses.
Or they had him: one of them would wait for him.
Her small black cape rested softly at the withers.
The Benedictines came when the Roman
army left. They brought bells with them, and time.
The horse he loved best, bowing the head. In blinders
at a trot she circled back when he was gone.

## The Long Answer

It's now so late,
    the two men
seated in the middle

of the frozen escalator
    on Connecticut Avenue,
underground,

can take their time
    to weld the one
thing to another

thing, anonymous
    and slow. Their heads
almost touch. The sun-

surface flash of the rod
    is not to be gazed into.
In their masks

they resemble
    the gods at Easter Island,
as under the stairs

I see a small hatch
    has been opened
where the guts

of the moving tread-
    mill are exposed.
They say nothing

to each other. They
    stare down at the work
of making things

work. They will not even
    show their surprise
when the slats,

one folding out
    of the next, begin
to rise as steps

that they will open
    to us, that we will ride
into the dome

of summer,
    like the answer
to a question

so old, no one
    can say what was asked
in the first place—:

and which leaves
    us, on the tip of
night's tongue,

sleepy and arriving
    in waves of heat,
with only each other,

on Connecticut
    Avenue, come out
from underground.

\*

To so many I am grateful for encouragement and support, but especially the editors, teachers, and judges who took interest in my writing early on, including Eleanor Wilner, Mary Oliver, Herb Scott, Jim Barnes, Kim Kolbe, Bill Olsen, Yusef Komunyakaa, Bruce and Jean Condo Weigl, Carolyn Forché, David Wojahn, Ilya Kaminsky, Carsten René Nielsen, Jericho Brown, Dick Wertime, Laren McClung, Kermit Moyer, Dave Mason, and Daniel Slager and my friends at Milkweed. To Blas Falconer for early friendship and collaborations. To Shawn Parell for our work embodying words and speaking asanas. To Judy Bowles who holds awareness in her own poems and within our community. Thanks to Kyle Dargan for our years of friendship and colleagueship. To Jim Youngerman, for collaborations on higher ground, as well as to Jane, Dori, and the Daves S. To Mark Irwin, for his careful eye and impeccable input. My thanks to my late parents who brought me to myself, though it meant losing their me. Finally, abiding gratitude to my family and extended family of truly sensational colleagues and friends, to Laura Denardis for the music, and to my sister, Dana, for our sharing.

Poems in this collection appeared originally in *Agni*, *The American Poetry Review*, *The Academy of American Poets Poem-a-Day*, *The American Reader*, *Berkeley Poetry Review*, *Blackbird*, *The Chariton Review*, *The Chattahoochi Review*, *Copper Nickel*, *Crazyhorse*, *The Florida Review*, *Gettysburg Review*, *Nimrod*, *The Pinch*, *Ploughshares*, *Poetry International*, *Prairie Schooner*, *Rosebud*, *Southern Humanities Review*, *Tinderbox*, *Virginia Quarterly Review*, *War Literature and the Arts*, *The Writer's Almanac*, and *Zone 3*.

About the Author

David Keplinger is the author of several collections of poetry, most recently *Another City* (Milkweed Editions, 2018), which was awarded 2019 UNT Rilke Prize. Among his other collections are *The Most Natural Thing* (New Issues, 2013) and *The Prayers of Others* (New Issues, 2006), which won the Colorado Book Award. His first book, *The Rose Inside,* was selected by Mary Oliver for the 1999 T.S. Eliot Prize. He teaches at American University in Washington, D.C.

www.ingramcontent.com/pod-product-compliance
Lightning Source LLC
Chambersburg PA
CBHW060526080526
44586CB00012B/630